Carving Blockheads

by

Stephen H. Prescott

FOX BOOKS
Fox Chapel Publishing Co Inc.

Fox Chapel Publishing Co., Inc.
PO Box 7948
Lancaster, PA 17603-7948

© 1996 by Fox Chapel Publishing

Publisher: Alan Giagnocavo
Project Editor: Ayleen Stellhorn
Electronic Editor: Robert Altland, Altland Design
Cover Photography: Bob Polett

ISBN # 1–56523–069–8

To order your copy of this book,
please send check or money order
for cover price plus $2.50 to:

Fox Chapel Book Orders
Box 7948
Lancaster, PA 17604–7948

Try your favorite book supplier first!

Table of Contents

Introduction by Bob Travis iv

Foreword by Stephen H. Prescott v

Chapter 1
Wood, Tools and Sharpening 1

Chapter 2
The Basic Blockhead Pattern 4

Chapter 3
Carving the Basic Blockhead 6

Chapter 4
Carving Variations on the Basic Blockhead 10

Chapter 5
Blockhead Painting and Finishing Tips 13

Chapter 6
Fifty-one Blockhead Projects 16

Chapter 7
Blockhead Props 42

Guest Carver Photo Gallery 46

Afterword 48

Introduction

I am honored and flattered to have been asked to write this introduction. Honored, because I consider Steve Prescott to be one of the finest carvers and instructors in America. Flattered because I have looked up to him for many years. Although I had known of Steve for quite some time, I did not meet him in person until the Fall of 1990. We were part of a group of caricature carvers that got together in the back room of a local tool and lumber store in Ft. Worth, Texas, to discuss how we might capitalize on our common goal of promoting caricature carving on a national level. That meeting marked the beginning of The Caricature Carvers of America (CCA). Steve was one of the leaders in organizing the group and in establishing the guidelines for CCA. As a result, he was unanimously elected first president of CCA.

Steve needs little introduction to the wood-carving community. He has long been recognized as an outstanding carver of western humor and as an excellent instructor of caricature carving. Now this, his second book on caricature carving, follows the well received *Cowtown Carving* that was published two years ago. His carvings have claimed many ribbons in competitions, including several at the prestigious International Woodcarving Congress in Davenport, Iowa. His students, in carving workshops across the country, rate the "Gentle Giant" a top-notch instructor. In this book, as in *Cowtown Carving,* Steve's systematic approach to developing the project and his close attention to details clearly attest to his lifetime as an educator.

This book will fill a critical void for caricature carvers. Here, for the first time, is a book on caricature carving that introduces the carver to the concept of creativity. In short, you will be challenged to be creative, and that is what becoming a good carver is all about. The pattern is here to get you started, and Steve gives you step-by-step instructions for one version of the Blockhead, but the onus is on you to use your creative skills. Use Steve's ideas and suggestions to your advantage, but force yourself to grow as a carver by creating your own design. Don't be intimidated by this approach. I have often heard beginning carvers, and in some cases even relatively advanced wood carvers, comment that, "I don't have any artistic ability," or roughly translated, "I can't design a carving on my own." While that may be true for some, it doesn't have to be that way. Creativity can be learned. You just have to get started, and this book provides the impetus to get you started.

Bob Travis
Caricature Carvers of America
Chief of Education, The California Carvers Guild
Professor of Agronomy, University of California, Davis, California

Foreword

In my opinion, creativity and imagination in woodcarving are many times sadly lacking. As I attend woodcarving shows around the country, I see table after table of similar carvings. Most of these are from "how-to" carving books that all of us rely on as we begin carving. Is it any wonder that woodcarving is considered in many circles as a craft rather than an art? Creativity and originality are primary ingredients in any artistic endeavor.

When I teach woodcarving classes and seminars, I prefer to allow my students to select a project from a variety of subjects. This allows for the diversity of interests and abilities that are always present in each class situation. Teaching a variety of subjects makes for a more interesting, challenging day for the instructor, too. Of course, having enough blanks to fulfill these needs has always presented a bulky problem in packing, and invariably, some students will always ask for a blank that I do not have. So, I decided to design a universal blank that could be nearly anything to anybody at any level. This proved to be easier said than done.

I needed a simple, one-piece project that would be basic enough for a beginner yet have the potential to challenge the more advanced carvers in my classes. I also wanted a figure with a large head so that caricaturized facial features could be easily seen and emphasized. Realistic figures are about seven to eight heads in height. I wanted my universal caricature figure to be about six inches tall and about four heads tall. The end result was the BLOCK-HEAD pattern presented in this book.

My main purpose in writing *Carving Blockheads* is to show how any carver can modify a basic pattern to create an original woodcarving that is uniquely his own. In other words, I hope to teach you to be a more creative woodcarver.

Carving Blockheads is designed for carvers of all levels who have a little imagination and creativity. By varying the head, hats and hand positions, different figures can be created, and the variety can be endless, limited only by your own creativity and imagination. To get you started, I've included over 50 different BLOCKHEAD versions, plus many other interpretations in the "Guest Carvers Photo Gallery" found at the end of this book.

Carving Blockheads is organized in such a way to: 1) present the basic BLOCKHEAD pattern, 2) show a step-by-step explanation of the carving of a basic BLOCKHEAD pattern and some variations, 3) present over 50 different BLOCKHEADS with a brief description of each version, 4) show additional BLOCKHEAD ideas from other carvers in the Guest Carver Photo Gallery.

Carving Blockheads can provide many hours of fun, entertainment and carving pleasure for caricature carvers of all levels.

Stephen H. Prescott
Fort Worth, Texas

Chapter 1

Wood, Tools and Sharpening

ALL OF THE BLOCKHEADS IN THIS BOOK HAVE BEEN carved from basswood. Kiln-dried, northern basswood is my first choice. Try to select clear, white basswood with little or no visible grain. All things being equal, I prefer a hard piece of wood to one that is on the soft side. It will hold detail better and leave shiny, clean tool cuts. Softer basswood is great when roughing out a piece, but tends to push and tear when you get down to carving the details. Avoid southern basswood, which is generally soft and spongy, and air-dried basswood, which is often old and very hard. If you have been carving very long at all, you probably have bought some "great deals" on basswood that turned out to be more work and effort to carve than they were worth. Buy quality basswood; the carving will be more fun, and the end product more pleasing.

Photo 1:1. *The BLOCKHEADS in this book were carved using the tools shown above. From left to right, they are a bench knife, a small v-tool, a $1/4$" veiner, a $3/16$" veiner, a $1/2$" shallow gouge, a strop and a diamond hone. Remember to wear a safety glove for your protection when using these tools.*

TOOLS
The BLOCKHEADS in this book can be carved with the following sharp tools (Photo 1:1): A bench knife with a straight cutting edge, a small v-tool palm chisel, a $1/4$"–$3/8$" 60-degree v-tool palm chisel, a $3/16$"–$1/4$" veiner (a deep u-gouge) palm chisel, and a $1/4$"–$3/4$" shallow gouge palm chisel.

These are also the tools that I recommend for those who are new to caricature carving. I have several large tool boxes full of tools, but these are the ones I keep coming back to and find myself using most of the

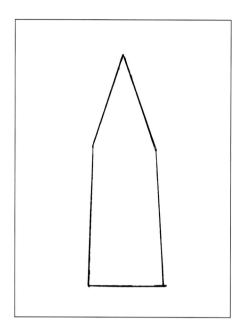

Figure 1.1 (above) shows how the bevel on a utility blade is shaped. Figure 1.2 and 1:3 (below) show how the bevel on a carving blade should be shaped. Most knives come with a factory edge that is not sharp nor beveled correctly for carving basswood. The bevel can be changed by honing the blade.

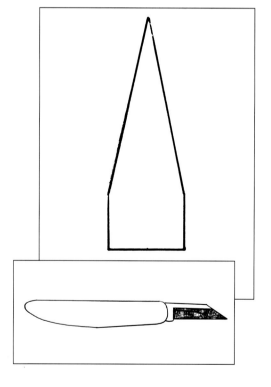

time. If you've been a student in one of my classes, you've probably heard me say about tools, "It's not the tool–it's the toolee." With enough talent and skill, you can make any tool work wonders. If you don't believe me, just watch caricature carvers Harold Enlow or Dave Dunham work their magic with a few tools from a small, beat-up, cardboard box.

SHARPENING

I'm convinced there are as many ways to sharpen as there are carvers. Sharpening is always a topic of conversation wherever carvers gather. Someone is always promoting a "new and improved" method of sharpening. Most carvers don't stay with a proven method long enough to learn the skill of sharpening properly. It's a hard, dirty, thankless job, but invest the time to do it right, and you'll find it's well worth the effort.

I've been using the following method for many years and don't want to change. I believe the old saying, "If it ain't broke, don't fix it." Eventually you'll become comfortable with a sharpening method, too.

Most of the time I use a 2" x 6" diamond hone. A hone is a piece of steel in which industrial-grade diamonds are imbedded. I prefer the diamond hone because it is small, light-weight, doesn't require water or oil, keeps its shape, doesn't wear out, and is easily transportable.

I also use a homemade leather strop, which is just a piece of scrap leather glued to a thin board (Photo 1:1). I apply jeweler's rouge or "zam" to the strop as a polishing compound. The rouge will remove the scratches left by the hone and the "wire edge burr" that develops right before the edge is sharp. When in my home shop, I use a buffing wheel charged with the same polishing compounds instead of the leather strop to remove the scratches left by the diamond hone.

Stropping should be done frequently during the carving process. A little preventative maintenance of stropping often saves a lot of time sharpening. Oftentimes, stropping is all that is necessary to restore an edge.

KNIVES

Most carving knives come with a factory edge that is not sharp, nor do they have the correct bevel for carving basswood. The bevel on a carving knife should be quite different than that on a pocketknife. The pocketknife is meant to have a utility blade bevel (Figure 1:1) capable of withstanding abuse that would damage the blade bevel on a carving knife (Figure 1:2).

A carving knife's blade bevel should ideally extend from the sharp edge all the way to the back edge of the blade (Figure 1:3). This bevel is achieved by laying the blade flat on the hone. It may require some time to shape the bevel correctly on a new blade.

Once the correct carving bevel has been achieved, begin to push the sharpened edge the full length of the hone, keeping it as flat as possible. Sharpen both sides equally. Work to achieve a "wire edge."

When the burr or wire edge is felt or seen under strong light, it's time to strop the blade. Pull the blade on the hand strop (sharp edge trailing, opposite of pushing on the hone). Keep the blade flat to prevent rounding the sharp edge. This is especially critical if you are using a power buffing wheel, which tends to round edges very quickly if buffed improperly.

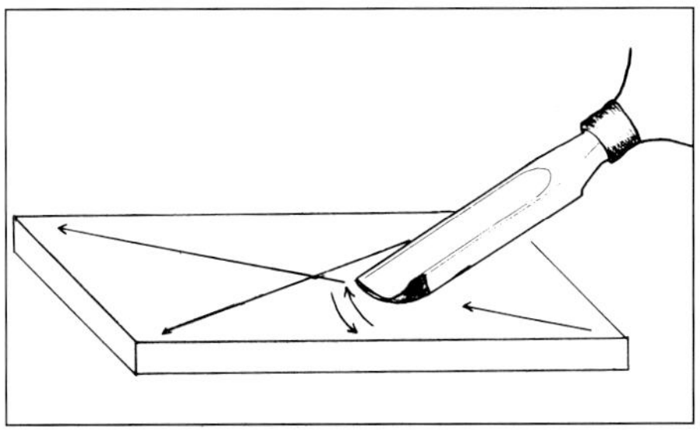

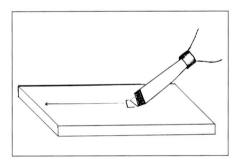

Figure 1:4. *Sharpen the outer edges of a gouge with a twisting motion. The inside edges of a gouge need not be touched unless they are damaged or misshapen.*

GOUGES

Sharpen gouges by starting at one corner edge and pushing forward with a twisting motion to the opposite corner. Then repeat the movement, going from the opposite corner (Figure 1:4). Alternate sides until the wire edge or burr is visible on the inside of the gouge. Buff the inside and outside until you have removed the wire edge. I rarely ever do anything to the inside of a gouge unless it's damaged or misshapen.

V-TOOLS

V-tools seem to pose the greatest sharpening problems for most people. Sharpen a v-tool as you would a knife with two edges. Push the blade, being careful to keep the edge flat on its bevel. Alternate sides and examine the bevel regularly to be certain that you are removing an equal amount from each side (Figure 1.5). Buff back and forth to remove the wire edge burr that will show on the inside edge. The trick to sharpening v-tools is to be patient and go slow. I much prefer the larger 60-degree v-tools. They can cut as fine a v-line as the smaller v-tools and are much easier to sharpen.

Figure 1:5. *Larger v-tools are easier to sharpen and often give the same cut as the smaller, harder-to-sharpen v-tools.*

SHARPENING SUMMARY
•Be patient.
•Check the bevel often and keep the bevel flat.
•Use a good strong light to see the wire edge or dulled bevel. (Magnifying glasses or an Opti-Visor will help if your vision is not what it once was.)
•Use the hand strop or power buffer to "finish off" the blade.
•Use the strop often while carving to maintain your edge.
•Again, be patient.

Chapter 2

The Basic Blockhead Pattern

The BLOCKHEAD was designed to allow each of my carving students to express his or her own creativity. From this one pattern, carvers can create any number of projects. The blocky head allows plenty of wood for carving a large head and different hats or for turning the head. The large amount of wood left in the hand area allows for a wide variety of hand and arm positions. With a pattern like this, your only limitations are your own imagination and creativity.

The basic BLOCKHEAD pattern is used for all of the projects in this book (Figure 2:1). The only variations from that pattern are the School Teacher, the Nurse, the Witch, the Wizard, the Cavewoman and Friar Tuck, which do not have wood removed between the legs to accommodate for a dress, gown or robe. The basic pattern requires a block 7" x 3^1/$_2$" x 2^1/$_2$". All of the BLOCKHEADS in this book have been carved from basswood.

You can easily enlarge or reduce the basic BLOCKHEAD pattern by using a copy machine that has those capabilities. Photocopying a pattern and enlarging or reducing single copies for your own personal use are not violations of this book's copyright and are permissible. However, duplicating the pattern for distribution or sale is a violation of copyright law.

If you do not have access to a bandsaw or prefer to work from dupli-carved rough-outs, they are available from the following suppliers: **Cowtown Carving Company,** Steve and Pat Prescott, 5812 Lalagray Lane, Fort Worth, Texas 76148, (817) 498–8144 or **Rossiter Ruff-outs** and Carving Supply, 1447 South Santa Fe, Wichita, Kansas 67211, (800) 8BLANKS.

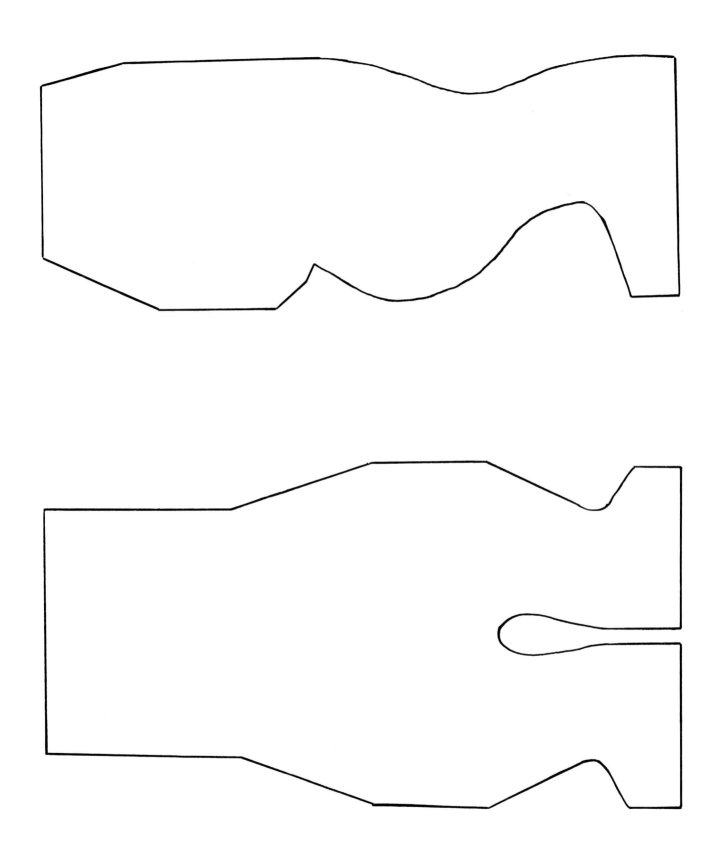

Chapter 3

Carving the Basic Blockhead

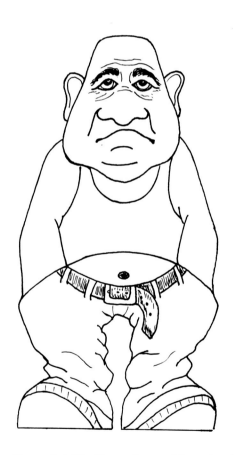

Figure 3:1 *The Grump is one of the easiest projects to carve. This illustration is meant to show details and is not intended to be used as a pattern. The basic BLOCKHEAD pattern appears on page 5.*

I WILL USE ONE OF THE SIMPLEST BLOCKHEAD projects to illustrate the basic step-by-step instructions. I've named him "The Grump." There is no hair to carve; he has both hands in his pockets; his expression is rather bland; his clothing is plain and simple; there are no props to carve... In short, he's just your typical guy, a good beginning project.

We will tackle the project in this order: 1) Preliminary steps, 2) setting in the head, 3) body shaping, 4) facial detail, and 5) final details. Painting, finishing and mounting will be addressed in Chapter 5.

Try the Grump first, even if you feel you are carving on a more advanced level. The other projects in this book have small variations and added props on this basic BLOCKHEAD pattern. These instructions can be applied to the BLOCKHEAD projects in Chapter 6.

Before beginning to carve your first BLOCKHEAD, observe the front view line drawing of the Grump (Figure 3:1). This line drawing is for detail reference only and is not intended for use as a pattern. Use the basic BLOCKHEAD pattern that appears on page 5.

PRELIMINARY STEPS
Basswood has been used for all of the BLOCKHEADS in this book. You may use other wood, if you prefer. You'll need a block of wood 7" x 3^1/$_2$" x 2^1/$_2$". Lay out your pattern with the grain running up and down. Draw both the front and side views on the block of wood (Photo 3:1). When bandsawing two sides on a block, I often use masking tape to hold the pieces together while sawing the other side. This helps to keep the piece flat and perpendicular to the blade, which is much safer.

Compare the completed bandsaw blank to the rough-out blank and to the bandsaw blank that has preliminary rounding completed (Photo 3:2). The rough-out blank saves a great deal of time and energy—you can skip right past the pattern drawing, bandsaw and roughed-out steps. The disadvantage to rough-outs is that you have a limited amount of wood left for variations from the basic pattern. (See page 4 for names of suppliers who sell BLOCKHEAD rough-outs.)

I begin almost every carving by rounding with a large-blade bench knife. I work all over the piece, removing all of the machine marks and generally shaping and rounding. It's kind of a pet-peeve of mine, but I like to get all the machine marks off and get down to the "good wood" before drawing all over it. Just take off about $1/8$" to $1/4$" all the way around to accomplish this. The square corners may require a little more. If you are working from a dupli-carved rough-out blank, liken your actions to peeling a potato to get down to this point.

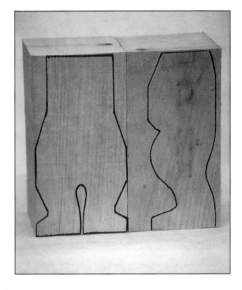

Photo 3:1. *Transfer the front and side views of the Grump onto a block of basswood 7" x 3$1/2$" x 2$1/2$".*

SETTING IN THE HEAD

The head shape for the Grump is pear-shaped; it is narrow at the top and wide at the bottom. There are lots of jowls, no neck and a double chin. Remember that the collar line should be higher in the back than in front and that it will disappear under the double chin. The head is completely bald, so the cranium will need to be carved down enough to make the ears stick out. Be sure to leave wood for the fat rolls on the back of the neck.

In the front, leave more wood at the bottom of the face for pouting lips, jowls and a double chin. Accent the width of the lower face by narrowing the temples and skull. The ears are large and are positioned on the back half of the head. The top arch of the ear is about even with the eyebrow. It joins the head about even with the corner of the eye. The ear extends down to the area between the bottom of the nose and top of the upper lip, depending on the amount of ear lobe you may have (Figure 3:2).

I usually block in the eye groove and nose mound at this point. Although I wait to do facial detail until last, I like to have the face and head framed-in for balance and proportion.

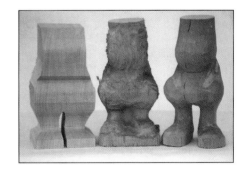

Photo 3:2 *shows a bandsaw blank on the left, a blocked-in bandsaw blank in the center, and a dupli-carved rough-out on the right. Using rough-out blanks save a great deal of time by allowing the artist to skip the pattern, bandsawing and roughing-out stages.*

BODY SHAPING

Don't worry about clothing or hem lines at this point. Just carve the basic shape with smooth, bold cuts that show the flow and shape of the body (Photos 3:6, 3:7, 3:8). The clothing details can be added later. Many of my students seem to lose their overall perspective when they are more concerned about where the sleeve ends or pant hems should be. At this point, think form, not detail. Narrow shoulders will accent

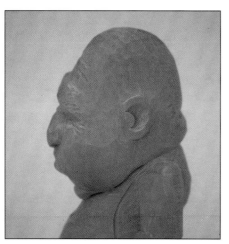

Photos 3:3, 3:4 and 3:5 *(above). Take a close look at the facial features of the Grump. Everything about his face should appear unhappy.*

the big head, wide belly and hips. The Grump has kind of a diamond shape to his body. Use a small v-tool to add detail to the T-shirt, jeans and shoes. The front of the T-shirt should be rising and the jeans sagging to expose his belly.

Tip: Most people use a v-tool to cut just a v-shaped groove in the wood. Learn to tilt the v-tool to the right or left cutting side to make an L-shaped cut. This makes a more perpendicular cut in the wood and catches light differently to create more dramatic shadow effects.

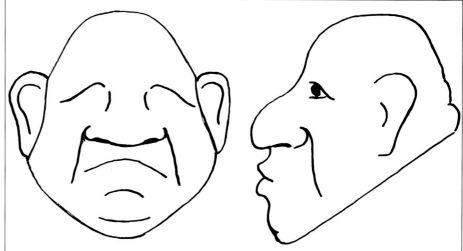

Figure 3:2 *shows an illustration of the front and side facial detail.*

FACIAL DETAIL

You should have already set in the facial planes early in the carving. All of the lines in the face should sag from the center down and outward to give the impression that the Grump is frowning and unhappy (Photos 3:3, 3:4, 3:5). Expressions are controlled by the angle of the eyebrows and the smile lines. The nose and eye shape have much less influence on expressions. The mouth and teeth are also an indicator of expression, but must be coordinated with the smile lines.

The nose planes are easily visualized if you think of them as a flat-topped pup tent (Figure 3:3). Round the wings with your v-tool or knife tip. Form the nostrils with your knife or a small gouge. Be careful not to break the wings of the nose when using the gouge. I've done this so many times that I almost always use my knife tip instead.

The eyes for the Grump are what I call "The Old Bagged Eye" (Figure 3:4).

Deepen the smile line at the corner of the nose and less deeply as the fat jowls blend into the neck. This will help form the mound on which we will carve frowning lips. The mouth is most easily carved if you think of the lips as being five distinct planes—two upper planes and one larger lower center plane with two smaller planes on each side (Figure

3:5). Blend the planes into each other to form the lips. Create a corner shadow by removing a small triangle from the corners of the lower lips. To give him that pouting look, leave the lower lip full and remove wood from under the lip with a small veiner (deep u-gouge). Smooth and blend the surface with your knife blade or small shallow gouge.

Photo 3:6, 3:7 and 3:8 (*above*). *These three photos show a comparison between a smooth body (on the left) and a detailed body (on the right).*

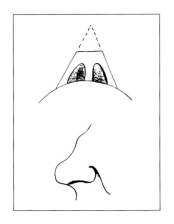 

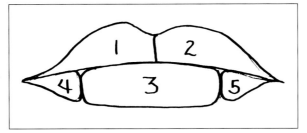

Figures 3:3, 3:4 and 3:5. *These illustrations show details of the Grump's nose, eyes and mouth.*

FINAL DETAILS

The Grump's pants are really drooping. This figure has little or not buttocks, short bowed legs, and large feet. These factors will necessitate lots of wrinkles in the crotch, behind the knees and above the insteps.

Because the face is rather pudgy, you'll only need wrinkles at the corners of the eyes. A couple of wrinkles across the forehead would be appropriate too.

Underscore the double chin line and round the fat roll on the back of the neck with a v-tool or knife. Blend them with a gouge at their outer edges.

Photo 3:9 *shows the completed, unpainted Grump. Painting and finishing instructions follow in Chapter 5.*

Chapter 4

Carving Variations on the Basic Blockhead

IF ALL OF THE CARVINGS IN THIS BOOK CAME FROM the same pattern, why do they all look different? The differences are small but can have dramatic results.

Variations on the basic BLOCKHEAD account for the uniqueness of each figure. These variations may include head or face shapes, head direction, hair styles, various hats, hand positions, clothing and props. By simply not removing the wood between the legs, figures with dresses, gowns or robes can be carved.

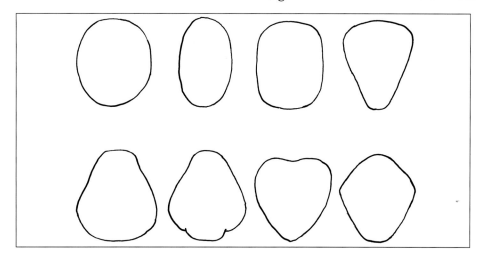

Figure 4:1 *shows outlines of the eight variations of BLOCKHEAD face shapes. The author prefers pear-shaped faces, though he uses many throughout this book.*

HEAD, FACE VARIATIONS

I prefer large heads on my BLOCKHEADS, but their heads can be any size or shape. Smaller heads are more appropriate with figures that have large hats or "big hair." My favorite head shape for BLOCKHEADS is pear-shaped although you may also use round, long ovals, diamonds and many others (Figure 4:1).

Head direction also makes a great difference. Heads can be straight ahead, turned to the right or left, or looking up or down. To see what a change in character a different head direction can make, compare two BLOCKHEADS with different head directions.

Hats, caps and hair styles are endless variations that will add uniqueness to your BLOCKHEAD. I highly recommend Claude Bolton's book *Heads, Hats and Hair* or Jack Hamm's *Cartooning the Head and Figure* as excellent sources for ideas.

HAND VARIATIONS

One of the comments I frequently hear about BLOCKHEADS is, "Why are the hands so large?" They are large, but they are actually in proper proportion to the large head. Realistic head to hand proportion is that the hand from the butt of the palm to the tip of the longest finger is about equal to the distance from the base of the chin to the normal hairline. Place your hand on your face and you'll see what I mean. (Note: My fellow carvers with receding hairlines should not try this.) A basic rule of thumb (no pun intended) for hand proportion is 4:3:2:1. The back of the hand being 4, the first set of finger bones being 3, the next set 2, and the last set 1 (Figure 4:2).

Hands are fairly easy to carve if you block in the hand mass in planes first. Don't worry about the individual fingers until after the hand planes are blocked in.

The hands in this book can be grouped into about six different variations. They are: 1) Hands in pockets, pants or jacket; 2) Clenched or grasping; 3) Palm up, holding objects; 4) Palm down, holding objects or resting; 5) Fingers open; 6) Thumbs in belt.

Hands in pockets

By far the easiest hands to carve, these are just large bulges under the clothing. Allow the wood "material" to "stretch" up to the high point of the knuckles. Don't worry about the pocket seam. Just carve the hand bulge from pants or jacket, over the hand and into the wrist/forearm area in one long stroke if the wood grain will allow it. The pocket seam or wrist cuff can be added later with a small v-tool.

Clenched or grasping

The hands are easily modeled by looking down on your own hands held in this position. A common carving mistake is to carve the inside finger planes too long in proportion to the outside planes. The inside area is really nothing more than a series of folds or wrinkles in the clenched fist and is opened only slightly when grasping an object (Figure 4:3).

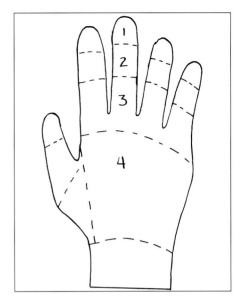

Figure 4:2. The human hand is proportional. Follow a ratio of 4:3:2:1 as shown in the illustration above when carving and detailing hands.

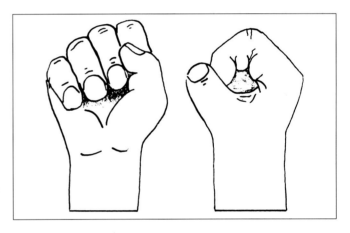

Figure 4:3. A clenched or grasping hand.

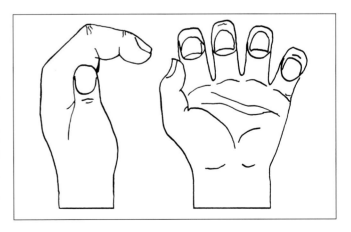

Figure 4:4. A palm-up hand.

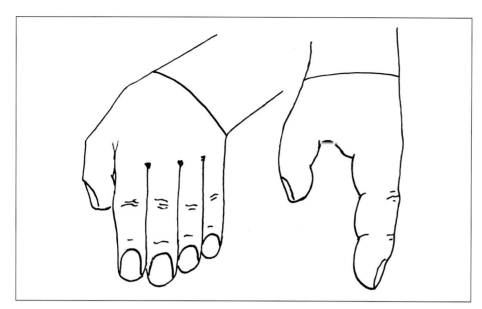

Palm Up

Basic hand and finger planes apply here, too, with the fingers conforming somewhat to the objects being held (Figure 4:4). The fingers are usually spread for larger objects and cupped for smaller ones. The Basketball Player, Volleyball Player and Woodcarver have this type of hand.

Palm Down

This style of hand is effective for caricature carvings but is not anatomically possible unless you have a broken wrist (Figure 4:5). It looks great when viewed from the front but is less believable when viewed from the side. It is better if the hand is in a parallel line with the forearm, but you have limited amount of wood to lay this out with the Basic BLOCKHEAD Pattern. The fingers and thumb are parallel. The Cowboy's hand resting on the gun holster and the Coach holding an object (page 22) are two examples.

Figure 4:5. A palm-down hand.

Fingers open

These hands are a sideways version of the palm-up hand. The palm is open and the fingers and thumb are spread. They should be angular and show some degree of tension. They may be turned palm-up, like the hands on the Fisherman (page 25), or palm-in, like the hands on the Carpenter (page 19) and the Mechanic (page 16).

Thumbs in belt or pocket

This hand is just a clenched fist with the thumb tucked behind the belt or into the pocket (Figure 4:6). Most of the last two finger bones are hidden under the hand, but the full index finger can be seen.

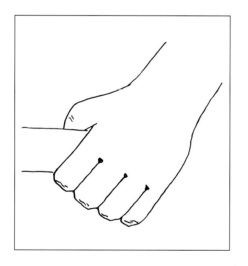

Figure 4:6. This type of hand is perfect for a caricature who has his thumb hooked in a belt or pocket.

In theory, hands should be the easiest body part to carve. After all, we have two ever-ready models right at the end of our arms. It's not like trying to look at your ears. Use your own hands as models, and observe their planes. Observing your hand planes and then carving each one carefully will produce better results. Remember to think of form rather than detail–planes rather than individual finger detail.

Chapter 5

Blockhead Painting and Finishing Tips

PAINTING

I use acrylics to paint my caricatures. I use Ceramcoat by Delta Artist's Acrylic Paints. This brand of acrylic paints is available in most arts and crafts stores.

The key to painting caricatures is to use plenty of water to dilute the paint so that the effect is like a stain or wash rather than a painted ceramic. The woodgrain should show through the stain so that there is no doubt that this is a woodcarving.

The list of colors in the Ceramcoat by Delta line at the left represents the colors that I have used to paint the BLOCKHEADS in this book. These colors represent only about one-third of the colors available from this manufacturer (Photo 5:1). I have used these acrylic paints for about ten years and heartily recommend them to my students. They are inexpensive and easy to mix and dilute. The small two-fluid ounce bottles are convenient to use. A small amount of paint can be mixed with water, and even the diluted paints will store well. They have the best flesh colors available—about six different shades. Since I have never been able to mix good flesh colors, this really is helpful. They also make an Acrylic

Photo 5:1 *shows the artist's collection of Ceramcoat paints, a type of acrylic paint manufactured by Delta.*

The author uses the following Ceramcoat paints to complete the BLOCKHEAD projects in this book:

2022 Antique Gold
2006 Avocado
2015 Purple
2023 Brown Iron Oxide
2025 Burnt Umber
2026 Orange
2029 Caucasian Flesh
2030 Burnt Sienna
2039 Cosmos Blue
2042 Pumpkin
2043 Tangerine
2050 Mocha
2054 Golden Brown
2055 Autumn brown
2057 Quaker Grey
2096 Dark Forest
2100 Woodland Night
2104 Fjord Blue
2108 Palomino
2126 Medium Flesh
2127 Dark Flesh
2133 Cape Cod
2405 Dusty Mauve
2418 Laguna
2424 Bambi
2436 Charcoal
2459 Crocus Yellow
2477 Denim Blue
2503 Bright Red
2505 White

 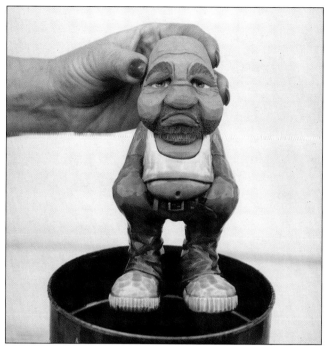

Photo 5:2 and Photo 5:3 show how the antiquing mixture is applied to the painted carving after the acrylics have dried. The antiquing mixture, a combination of burnt umber paint and boiled linseed oil, tones down the colors of the paint, brings out the wood grain, and seals the wood.

Satin Varnish that can be used on painted eyes to give them a realistic shiny appearance. It can also be used on glasses or goggles for the same effect.

FINISHING

To finish my carvings, I use an antiquing solution of boiled linseed oil and burnt umber artist oil paint. I don't have an exact measured formula, but I usually mix one to two inches of paint from the tube in about a quart of boiled linseed oil. I dip the piece in a coffee can of the antiquing solution (Photos 5:2 and 5:3) and wipe off the excess with a paper towel. The purpose of the antiquing is to tone down the colors, bring out the woodgrain, and seal the wood.

Warning—The boiled linseed solution is flammable, and the paper towels or other cloths you use to wipe excess solution off the caricature are combustible. Store used materials in an airtight container.

I rarely wax my carvings, but I have several caricature carver friends that get excellent results by using a liquid wax instead of the antiquing solution. Most come in natural and dark stains. The two can be mixed for an in-between stain. The wax finish is very good for carvings that are handled frequently, and they can be rewaxed and re-buffed to restore the finish.

MOUNTING

While most all of these BLOCKHEADS will stand balanced on their own because they have rather large feet, I usually mount them on a base anyway. This gives them added protection and a nice finished look. A $1/4$–inch dowel in the foot and base (Photo 5:4) works much better than gluing two flat surfaces to secure the carving to the base. Be careful not to drill too deeply into the foot, or you can ruin a nearly completed carving.

Photo 5:4 *(above) shows how the finished carving is mounted to the base with a dowel. The carving will stand on its own, but the author finds the pieces are much more stable when mounted on a base.*

Photo 5:5 *The finished carving.*

Chapter 6

Fifty-one Blockhead Projects

Initially, this book started with only twenty projects. As I displayed these first 20 BLOCKHEADS, I received many enthusiastic responses and many more suggestions for potential projects. The size of the book increased to 35 projects, and then to 50. I just had to cut it off somewhere. I could have carved many more, and so can you. That's the purpose of this book–to teach and stimulate creative ideas from one basic pattern. Even with these BLOCKHEADS, try to modify them to make each one your own. Push yourself to try new ideas with these basic patterns, and you'll find yourself growing as a caricature carver.

I've organized the 51 BLOCKHEAD projects according to alphabetical order, not necessarily in the order of their difficulty or complexity. Those projects with an asterisk would be appropriate for beginning carvers.

Auto Mechanic

IN THE COLLECTION OF KAITLYN R. AND AMANDA S. LECLAIR, WICHENDON, MA

Probably one of your most anxious moments is when you must leave one of your most valuable possessions, your automobile, in the hands of someone who looks like this guy. Finding a trustworthy, competent auto mechanic can be as big a problem. You can't tell by looking. Most mechanics do not "dress for success," and many don't always exhibit the best of personal hygiene. I guess those qualities are not in the job description anyway. Bubba's appearance does not exactly build confidence, but this BLOCKHEAD can get the job done.

Bubba's gimme cap is on backwards, the brim against the back of the neck. Hair is sticking out of the vent in the front. The head is turned to the left. The left hand is opened to hold the repair bill. The right hand is clenched to hold the wrench, his universal repair tool.
Props: Wrench, repair bill.
Finish: Coveralls and cap, Navy blue. Shoes, black. Hair, brown.

Barnstormer Pilot*

This is one of the first BLOCKHEADS I carved, and he is rather basic. This old fellow appears to be daydreaming about long-gone days of glory and the adventure of flying in an open cockpit. This balanced figure with straight head, hands in pockets, and feet even make this a pretty easy carving to execute.

Begin by forming the leather aviator's helmet. Although I didn't carve him with goggles on top of the helmet, that would be a good touch. Next form the scarf around his neck. The hands go in the leather jacket pockets. The riding pants have flared thighs and are stuffed into high stove-top boots. The face is rather expressionless. The eyes have drooping eyelids. The mouth is almost covered by the thick moustache.
Props: None.
Finish: Boots and helmet, dark brown. Jacket, brown. Pants, tan. Scarf, red.

Baseball Player

What's more American than baseball? This ball player is stereotypical in that he has the obligatory chew of tobacco and beard stubble. He appears to be a pitcher checking the first-base runner or getting the signal from the catcher, although he could represent any field position. I've painted him as one of our local professional baseball teams (some may debate the use of the word professional here), but he can be painted to represent any team you wish.

Turn the head a quarter turn to the left. Accent the mouth and chew by shifting the mouth and half an eye to the left and up. Caricaturize the cap by making it extra small, thereby emphasizing the large face. The right hand is a palm-up, holding-type hand with a ball in it, and the left hand has a glove on it.
Props: Ball, glove.
Finish: Baseball uniform of your choice. Baseball, white. Hair and glove, brown.

Basketball Player

This BLOCKHEAD may not be politically correct, but in the art of caricature, just about anything goes. (You should see how I caricaturize a Caucasian basketball player—super skinny, pale white, and leggy to the point of clumsiness.)

A lot of wood needs to be removed to make this figure appear tall. Note that the facial features and underlying bone structure of African-Americans are different than Caucasian features: The skull has a less prominent brow ridge and a flatter nose bridge; the oral mound and teeth are more prominent; and the mandible (jawbone) is smaller. Facial features to emphasize include wide-open eyes, a round, flattened nose, full lips and small ears. The right hand is a palm-up, holding hand with spread fingers. The left is a relaxed hand. The legs are skinny with knobby knees and the feet are big

Props: Basketball.

Finish: Basketball uniform of your choice. Fleshtone, medium flesh #2126 mixed with Burnt Umber #2025.

Boxer

This pugilist, believe it or not, was the winner. You can tell by his victorious smile that he won the fight, but unfortunately, he took his lumps in the process. I guess lumps, bumps, bruises and swelling are a part of boxing, just as cuts and bandages are a part of caricature carving.

This BLOCKHEAD has a large pear-shaped head. The large ears are accentuated by the bald head. Take care in laying out the uneven brow line and eye groove that forms the closed, swollen eye and the compensating wide-open eye. Be sure to add the missing tooth and flattened, wrinkled nose. Skinny, spindly legs contrast with large, high-top boots. Leave as much wood as possible to form the boxing gloves, which are not much different than enlarged clenched-type hands without the fingers.

Props: None.

Finish: Tank top, white. Trunks, red. Shoes, black.

Canadian Mountie

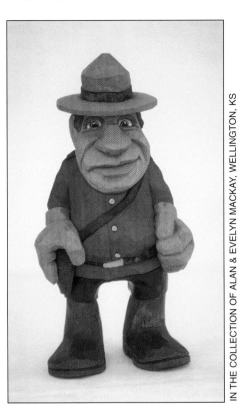

This was an early BLOCKHEAD that I carved in preparation for a seminar I was teaching in Edmonton. The Mounties have an outstanding reputation for honesty, integrity and always getting their man. Probably they are just Texas Rangers who have strayed across the Red River. The "Smokey the Bear" hat is the most distinctive part of this carving.

I used my bandsaw to cut in above and below the straight hat brim. Be careful not to thin this brim too early because it will be fragile. Block in the pear-shaped head with a strong jaw line. The left hand is a closed/clenched fist. The right hand is resting over the holster. The flared thigh pants are stuffed into stove-top boots. The face is fairly ordinary with a wide smile. Hair should be a short military-style cut.

Props: None.

Finish: Pants and hat, tan. Boots and holster, dark brown. Coat, red.

IN THE COLLECTION OF ALAN & EVELYN MACKAY, WELLINGTON, KS

Carpenter/Woodworker

My grandfather was a carpenter, and I remember, as a young boy, smashing my fingers with a hammer as I played in the shop. Here I am now, a grown man. I still love to play with wood, but my skill with a hammer is still infantile. This BLOCKHEAD has a swollen thumb and a great facial expression that seems to show pain, anger, surprise and disbelief all at the same time.

Block-in the head as a pear shape with a small skull and a large jaw. Focus all of the expression across the wrinkled bridge of the nose. The angle of the brow and bulging eyes and the angle of the distorted mouth all radiate from that center as well as the lines and wrinkles. The left hand is a clenched hand with the swollen thumb sticking up. The right hand is still grasping the hammer. The body is slim, which makes the arms appear tensed as they are held away from the body.

Props: Hammer.

Finish: Shirt, light blue. Pants, denim. Shoes, white.

COLLECTION OF LARRY & CAROL YUDIS, THE WOODCRAFT SHOP, BETTENDORF, IA

Caveman

The primitive cave dweller was not thought to possess a high intelligence. Everyday survival was his number-one priority. The big club was always close at hand for threats, reinforcement, hunting food, or hunting a mate.

Create a large pear-shaped head with a small skull cap (small brain capacity) and a massive undershot jaw. He should have a very heavy brow line, a sloping forehead, a large, flat nose, and small ears. I gave mine one big tooth. I chose not to include hair on the upper lip to give him a more ape-like appearance. Carve the eyes as deeply as possible. The hands are grasping and clenched. The body hair was done with a wood burner although it could be textured with a small veiner or v-tool. The animal skin clothes were textured with a small veiner. The large areas of exposed skin require more skill and knowledge of muscle anatomy. Don't carve them straight like pipe cleaners. Give him some bulging muscles.

Props: Club.
Finish: Fur, brown. Hair, black.

Cavewoman

It has been theorized that the cavewoman was more advanced than the caveman. I'm sure that all you feminists would say that holds true for modern woman too. That debate has raged since the beginning of mankind (or is it womankind?). At least our cavewoman looks better and more intelligent than her counterpart.

Lots of unruly hair is a dominant feature to caricature here. Carving a feminine face is quite different than carving a masculine face. Features are smoother and less pronounced. There is very little brow ridge and the oral mound is more prominent. The eyes are usually larger and set a little wider than on the male. Carve the face as heart-shaped. Look in the Guest Carvers Photo Gallery for other examples of female faces. Plenty of wood will need to be removed to bring out the baby. The left arm is tense and held away from the body.

Props: None.
Finish: Clothing, dark brown. Hair, straw.

Civil War Soldier

Blue vs. Gray, North vs. South, brother vs. brother—a horrible time in our country's history. Yet it is also one of the most romanticized and glorified periods. This BLOCKHEAD can be carved as a Yankee or as a Reb. Those of you who don't like to carve eyes will find the low brimmed cap a relief. See Dave Dunham's Rebel in the Guest Carver's Photo Gallery for a neat alternative.

Begin by forming the cap that seems too small for the large head. He also has a very large nose that is partially covered by the cap brim. The beard is full and the mustache is neatly upswept. The hands are both clenched/grasping type. The left is resting on the sword sheath, which was carved separately. The sword is in the right hand. He is wearing oversized high-top boots with the toes pointed outward.

Props: Sword, scabbard (rifle, flag optional).

Finish: Uniform, blue with gold trim. Boots and belt, black. Hair, brown.

IN THE COLLECTION OF MELVIN L & JANET B. TITUS, ALBUQUERQUE, NM

Clown*

Everybody loves a clown. Clowns are a favorite subject for carvers and for collectors too. I guess that is true because whether they are in happy or sad face make-up, they always bring us smiles and laughter. The variety of costumes and make-up is unlimited, so you could carve a whole collection of these BLOCKHEADS.

The head and hair should be blocked-in as a long heart shape. Ears are optional depending on hair style. The large hands are in the pockets of the oversized jump suit, giving the body a large diamond shape. The ankles and legs are skinny, which will accent the large clown shoes. This BLOCKHEAD could be easily modified by having hands holding various props such as balloons, an umbrella, etc.

Props: (Balloon, umbrella, optional.)

Finish: Hair, orange. Jumpsuit, purple and yellow. Shoes, red and white. Flower, yellow and brown.

IN THE COLLECTION OF JOHN & CLAIRE MARINO, EVERETT, MA

Coach

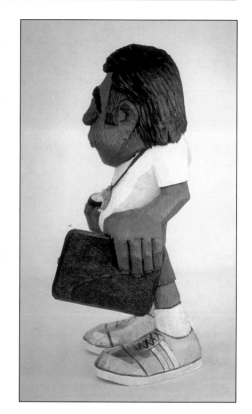

"There aren't but two kinds of coaches, those who have been fired and those that are going to be." Bum Phillips, Houston Oilers.

Having been a head football coach, I can really relate to that statement and to this caricature. His look of eager anticipation as he clocks 40-yard dash times reveals the eternal optimism that coaches must have in order to maintain some semblance of sanity.

The head is turned a quarter-turn to the right. The right hand is a palm-up, holding-type hand that supports the stopwatch. The left hand is a palm-down type holding a clipboard. Be sure to elevate the right eyebrow in the direction he is looking. The hair is Jimmy Johnson style, although a crew cut might be appropriate too. A baseball cap with a team logo might be a good addition.

Props: Clipboard (balls or athletic equipment optional).

Finish: T-shirt, socks and shoe, white. Shorts, gray. Hair and clipboard, brown. Shoes, blue.

Cowboy

Cowboys are a favorite subject of caricature carvers everywhere. They can be carved as mean, despicable characters or sweet, handsome dudes or honest, upright citizens. Our BLOCKHEAD cowboy is one of the good guys, even though he carries two six guns. He is fairly clean, neat and straight-forward, although you could certainly change his character to design your own cowboy.

I used my bandsaw to notch in above and below the front hat brim. Tilt the hat back on to the shoulders to gain more wood to form the hat. Notice that the mustache is raised on one side as if he's talking out of the side of his mouth. The hands are identical palms-down, grasping hands. The thumbs and fingers are draped over the pistols, revealing the hammer and holsters in front and below.

Props: (Chaps, rope, branding iron, optional.)

Finish: Shirt, green. Pants, denim blue. Boot and hat, brown. Bandanna, red.

Deep Sea Diver

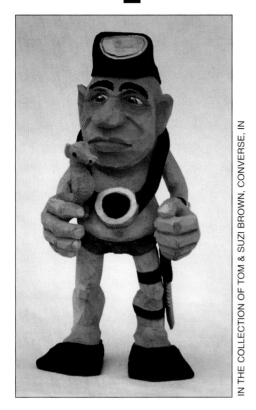

The diver, with his "Buoy-knife" and "horse," is really just a cowboy of the sea. He will require a little more skill to carve because he has little or no clothes that cover up his muscles.

The head is slightly turned to the right. Leave wood on top of the head to form the mask. Leave wood on the back for the air tank. (This could be an added piece if you prefer.) Set in the air hose and respirator. A large amount of wood must be removed for these items to be made more prominent. Carve the feet down flat to form the flippers. The right hand is a slightly opened, clenched fist. The left hand is a clenched fist.

Props: Knife, sea horse. (Air tanks, spear gun, optional).

Finish: Diving gear, tank, mask and flippers, black. Diving trim, silver. Trunks, purple. Clear fingernail polish is used on the glass of the face mask. Clear Varnish #7007 could also be used.

Dentist

Visits to the dentist do not usually bring back fond memories, even though today's modern dentistry techniques are relatively painless, except to your pocketbook. This BLOCKHEAD dentist has used a pair of pliers to remove a rather large tooth. The diopters on his head were a special request. (Kind of like Opti-visors for us woodcarvers.) He is dressed like most dentists in a lab coat, slacks and golf shoes.

Turn the head to the right and focus the expression on the tooth he has just pulled. His face can be whatever you want; I've chosen a slight, off-center grin, as if he is proud of his handiwork. The left hand is in his pocket and the right hand holds the pliers and tooth. The wingtip golf shoes are the two-tone wingtip style with tassels covering the laces.

Props: Diopters, pliers and tooth (drill and syringe optional).

Finish: Lab coat, white. Slicks, black. Golf shoes, black and white. Hair, gray.

Doctor

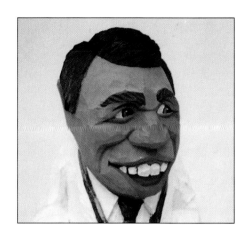

Contrary to what you see on the TV as you watch exciting medical dramas, the life of a physician can be fairly routine and sometimes boring. This doctor has a patient record folder and a pen with which he is prepared to record data. I guess every job has its obligatory paper work.

The head is turned to the left and has a full head of hair. The smiling mouth has a full set of teeth with the gums exposed. The eyes are turned to the left also. As a professional he is dressed in a shirt, tie and slacks although a lab coat would also be appropriate. Leave enough wood to form the stethoscope around his neck. The left hand grasps the pencil, and the right hand, with fingers and thumb partially extended, clamps the file folder or prescription pad. The legs and feet are ordinary except for their slight stagger.

Props: File folder, pen/pencil (prescription, optional).

Finish: Shirt, white. Tie, blue and yellow. Slacks, gray. Shoes, black. Hair, brown.

Fireman

It seems that at almost every show someone will ask if I have any firemen available. Firemen seem to be a favorite of both kids and adults. For those of you who want to sell your carvings, a fireman is a good piece to add to your repertoire. Maybe it's the danger or the excitement or the heroism of saving lives that appeals to us. My BLOCKHEAD fireman is fairly traditional in his long coat.

Begin by forming the helmet and head. The back brim of the helmet should extend over the shoulders. The ears can be covered or exposed depending on the helmet's style. The left hand is grasping/holding the hatchet. The right hand is holding the hose. It is a grasping-type hand, but turned at a different angle. The coat is only hip length on the dupli-carved blank. If you are using a bandsaw blank, you could make the coat longer by not cutting out as much wood between the legs.

Props: Axe, hose (flashlight, optional).

Finish: Helmet, yellow. Coat, pants and boots, black.

Fisherman

This happy bass fisherman is proudly displaying his trophy catch. Fishermen are as fanatical and enthusiastic as anyone you'll find in any hobby. His zeal is evident in the big smile exhibited here. Some good variations on this BLOCK-HEAD are a fly fisherman in waders or an empty-handed fisherman showing the size of "the one that got away."

This BLOCKHEAD is square and straight forward. Both hands and feet are the same and the head is straight ahead. The hands are palm-up, holding types. The fish I carved now appears rather stiff. It might look better if it were sagging in the middle and drooping on either end. The hat is a floppy canvas type. If you are really into detail, you might try carving some flies or lures on the hat. The sunglasses and fishing vest are part of the uniform. Denim jeans and tennis shoes complete the clothing.
Props: Big fish (rod and reel, minnow bucket, creel, tackle box, optional).
Finish: Vest and hat, tan. Jeans, denim. Shoes, white. Hair, brown. Use Acrylic Varnish #7007 on the sunglasses.

IN THE COLLECTION OF J. W. DAILY, LONGVIEW, TX

Football Player

Having spent a significant part of my life playing and coaching football, this BLOCKHEAD is one of my personal favorites. His face reflects the joy of victory as well as the wear and tear of the hard-fought contest. The uniform can be designed and painted to match that of your favorite team. Uniform style on my BLOCKHEAD just happens to be just like "America's Team."

The football player is straight forward and balanced. Both feet and both hands are the same. The face and helmet should be the main emphasis in this carving. The helmet looks best if it's tight and a little too small. Be sure to leave wood for the chin strap. The face is similar to the Boxer. The eyes, nose, and mouth are basically the same. A face mask can be added although this guy looks as if he never used one.
Props: Face mask (football, helmet or other equipment, optional).
Finish: Pants and helmet, silver. Shoes, jersey and trim, white. Trim, navy blue. Shoes and hair, black.

IN THE COLLECTION OF RAYMOND M. JONES, BUCHANAN DAM, TX

Frankenstein*

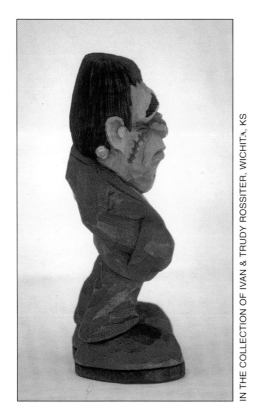

The science fiction horror film star, Frankenstein, has long captured the imagination of young and old alike. He is easily caricatured by exaggerating his square head, heavy brow line, deep set eyes and large jaw. Scars, neck bolt electrodes and death-warmed-over coloring add to the recognizable character.

Hands in the pockets and large simple boots make the body of Frankenstein pretty generic and relatively easy to carve. The face is the main feature on this carving. The upper head should be a little small (small brain capacity) and flat. Leave plenty of wood for the heavy brow, a large flattened nose, and a prominent jaw. The eyes should be carved as deeply as possible to accent the brow line even more. The ears are small. Leave wood under the ears for the neck bolt electrodes.

Props: None.

Finish: Clothing, varying shades of black. Hair, black. Flesh, accent with gray and green.

Friar Tuck

The Friar Tuck that I remember from the old Robin Hood movies was rarely a good example of a religious leader. In the movies, he was portrayed as a raucous, boisterous brawler who also had moral weaknesses in the areas of drunkenness and gluttony. Even with these character flaws, he was still an affable, good-hearted person. We'll try to make this monk a little more pious and respectable.

Do not remove wood between the legs on your basic BLOCKHEAD pattern in order to form the long robe. Block in a head that is round in shape. The head is bald with only a ring of hair. The ears are prominent. The nose is wide, as is his pleasant close-lipped smile. The hands are the same type. The left is more relaxed, and the right grasps his walking staff. The sandal-clad feet peek out from under the long robe.

Props: Walking staff/stick (turkey legs, tankard, optional).

Finish: Robe, brown. Rope, straw. Sandals, tan. Hair, gray.

Frontiersman

If you are a baby boomer, one of your favorite childhood heroes was most likely Davy Crockett. Even after nearly forty years, I bet some of you can still sing the theme song. And didn't we all look great in coon-skin caps?

As you block in the head and hat for this BLOCKHEAD, be sure to allow wood for the coon-skin cap's tail trailing over the shoulder. The head is turned slightly to the right. The eyes are turned to the right also. The mouth is clenching a Kentucky tobacco cigar. The hands are balanced grasping/clenched types. The left hand has the thumb on top. The right hand holds a large "Bowie knife." (I think I may have mixed my childhood heroes here.) The clothing is a buckskin outfit with fringe on the sleeves and pants. There is a sash tied around his waist.

Props: Knife, cigar, knife sheath (rifle and steel trap, optional).

Finish: Coon-skin cap, gray, white and black. Buckskin, tan. Sash, red. Hair, black.

IN THE COLLECTION OF JOHN & DIANE THOMPSON, BEAUMONT, TX

Golfer

Modern-day golfers dressed in bright, pastel-colored slacks, sport shirts and baseball caps are common sights on the golf course today. A nostalgic sight is PGA golfer Payne Stewart, who dresses in the old style of knickers, knee socks, sweaters and golf cap. This is the way I've chosen to show my golfer. The bent golf club is common to both eras.

The head is turned slightly to the right. Form the golf cap first. He has a somewhat quizzical expression as if he can't find his golf ball. The hands are identical except for the thumb positions. The right hand is the grasping type and the left hand is a grasping hand with a raised thumb to clamp the score card.

Props: Bent club, score card (golf bag, optional).

Finish: Golf cap, gray. Sweater, turquoise. Knickers and shirt, Palomino. Shoes, black and white. Socks, Argyle plaid.

IN THE COLLECTION OF MICHAEL D. FOX, FORT WORTH, TX

Hockey Player

I must admit, as a hot-weather Texan I didn't know too much about carving a hockey player. But since the Stars have moved into our area, things have changed dramatically. Now, all the kids have in-line skates and hockey sticks, and hockey leagues are forming all around town. This BLOCKHEAD hockey player captures the rougher spirit of hockey by sporting a black eye, missing teeth and flattened nose.

Form the helmet first. I like the headgear to be too small in comparison to the head and face, but you could make the helmet too large and be just as effective. Be sure to leave wood for the chin strap, or you'll have to carve it buckled under the chin. The hands are similar, with one opened slightly to hold the stick. The hand planes are obscured by the bulky, padded gloves. The skate boots will look better if carved a little narrower than regular BLOCKHEAD feet.

Props: Stick, blades.

Finish: Jersey, white. Pants, shoes and helmet, red.

Hunter

In recent years, hunters have taken considerable abuse from animal rights groups labeling them as Bambi killers or gun-toting NRA extremists. In reality, most are nature-loving conservationists who help control the balance of wildlife by hunting and paying license fees. Hunting is no longer a poor man's hobby. With clothing, equipment, hunting leases, and fees, hunters also contribute a lot of money to the economy. This hunter has the semi-official hunting uniform of a warm hat, boots, gloves, jacket and pants, all of which are in camouflage or fluorescent orange.

Block in the hat and head first. The face is ordinary. Beard stubble would be appropriate also. I chose to put a toothy smile on mine. The hands are bulky because of the gloves. The pants are stuffed into the high-top lace-up boots. The rifle is carved separately.

Props: Shot gun or rifle (bow and arrows, game, optional).

Finish: Coat, red plaid or orange. Pants, tan. Boots, brown. Hat, gray.

Indian Brave

Probably no other group has been more indelibly stereotyped than the American Indian. Hollywood's image of the noble savage with dominant cheekbones, a stoic expression, red skin, feathers and standard buckskin clothing is set in our minds. In reality, there is as much variety among Indians and their tribes as there is in any other population. In caricature, we strive to exaggerate the dominant traits, so this BLOCK-HEAD stresses those traits listed above.

As you block in the diamond-shape face, be sure to leave wood for the hair on both sides of the face. The face has drooping eyes, an expressionless mouth and lots of wrinkles. The small arms are bare except for arm bands. The buckskin pants have fringes down each leg. A breach cloth might be good here, too. War paint is a possibility as well. The hands are both tilted, grasping/holding types.

Props: Bow, arrows (tomahawk, quivers optional).

Finish: Head band, red, white and blue. Buckskin, tan. Moccasins, brown oxide.

Keystone Cop

Those old silent movies with the slapstick antics of the Keystone Cops are still considered to be comedy classics. Their inept style of law enforcement never hurt anyone but themselves; they never caught anybody either, always managing to bumble and stumble their way through each madcap adventure.

Form the domed helmet first. There is a slight flair at its base. He has no hair so that the ears protrude more noticeably. The dominant facial features are the round, bulbous nose and large, thick mustache. The eyes are open and alert. The left hand is a grasping/clenched type with a nightstick carved separately and added. The right hand is a palm down/holding type that is resting over the holster. there is a simple belt around the body. It does not have all the equipment attached to it as a modern policeman's belt would. The legs and feet are balanced.

Props: Nightstick.

Finish: Uniform, Navy blue. Shoes, belt and helmet, black.

Leprechaun

Leprechauns, four-leaf clovers and pots of gold are things of which fanciful dreams are made. Fact or myth, Leprechauns make great caricature carvings. Their twinkling eyes, mischievous grin and outlandish attire lend them to caricature. "Luck of the Irish" to you as you carve this fun BLOCKHEAD.

Form the small derby-style hat first. As you reduce the size of the head to fit under the hat, be sure to leave enough wood to form the pointed ears. The face has a short, upturned nose and large, toothy grin. The cheeks are pushed upward and the smiling eyes are almost squinted closed. The eyebrows are arched. The hands are almost identical. The left is lower and turned down. The right is higher and turned inward. The legs are very thin. The feet are staggered with the right being farther forward.

Props: Cane, four-leaf clover (pot of gold, optional).

Finish: Suit and hat, green. Socks and sweater, yellow. Shoes, black. Hair, orange.

Little Old Man

Little old men make neat caricature subjects. One of my favorite resource books for caricaturizing them is *Humans*, by Mike Dowdall and Pat Welch. In this book, the aging process is very well-illustrated in an entertaining, humorous way. I enjoy carving toothless old coots who are cantankerous enough in their old age not to care if they are toothless or if anyone else knows.

It may be helpful to bandsaw the profile of the face on this old fellow. Over time, the absence of teeth causes the nose and the chin to sag, almost to the point of joining. Exaggerate the sunken area of the missing dentures. The neck should be skinny and flabby. The body should be spoon-chested with a little pot belly, spindly arms and legs with large bony hands. The left hand is in his pants pocket. The right is a palm-down grasping type. The cane is carved separately.

Props: Cane.

Finish: Shirt, white. Pants, tan. Shoes, brown. Hair, white.

Lumberjack

A lumberjack is thought of as a big, rugged, outdoor type. The image of tall-tale woodsman, Paul Bunyon, is what we are looking for in this BLOCKHEAD. This lumberjack is still using old-style equipment–the ax. Typical clothing style here should include a plaid flannel shirt with long johns underneath, knit cap, gloves and high-top lace-up boots.

Block in the small cap and big head. A large, strong jaw with either beard stubble or full beard would be good. The arms and hands are balanced. Both hands are the clenched/grasping type. The ax and tree are carved separately and added. The lace-up boots are large with skinny ankles. Thick wool socks that are rolled over the top of the boots would be a good touch also.

Props: Ax, tree (chainsaw, optional).

Finish: Plaid shirt, red (plaid patterns drawn with Pentel ultrafine permanent pens). Long johns, parchment. Gloves, tan.

Magician

This little magician is one of my favorite BLOCKHEADS, probably because I haven't seen many carved magicians or maybe just because he has such a happy face that I can't help but smile when I look at him. His face has an ear to ear grin as if to show even he is amused that his trick of pulling a rabbit out of the hat really worked. His formal attire and neatly coiffured hair are stereotypical for an entertainer.

The magician's head is slightly turned to his left. Create a large, oval mound for the big toothy smile. Push the cheeks back into the face so the smile wraps around the mound. The cheeks are pushed upward so that the lower lids are almost straight. The eyebrows are arched to open the eyes. The right hand is grasping the wand, and the left hand is basically the same, but the thumb is raised from the fingers with hat brim fitted between them.

Props: Magic wand, rabbit in hat.

Finish: Shirt, white. Tuxedo, shoes, bow tie and hair, varying shades of black.

Modern Airplane Pilot

Think about the last time you flew on a commercial flight. Did you scrutinize the pilot very thoroughly? Did you check his credentials closely? Did you ask to see his license? Do you even know if he had a license? We certainly put a great deal of trust that everything will work out just fine at 35,000 feet and 400 mph. After thinking about these things, you will certainly be phobic if you weren't before. Actually, most pilots are accomplished professionals, and there is little to worry about. This BLOCKHEAD pilot is ready to go with his flight plan in hand.

The pilots hat should be blocked in first. This fellow has a large nose and thick mustache. The left hand is a grasping type with thumb raised to clamp down n the flight plan. The right hand is a grasping-type hand to hold the pull cord for a flight bag. The feet are slightly staggered.

Props: Flight plan, rolling flight bag.
Finish: Suit and cap, Navy blue or black. Shoes and suitcase, black.

Nurse

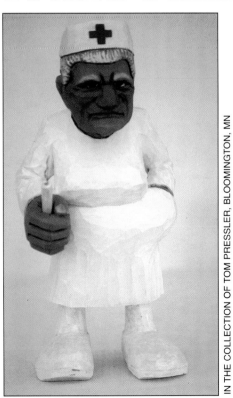

One of my favorite caricature carvings is Andy Anderson's carving scene of a doctor, nurse and patient. His nurse was easily one of the ugliest women ever carved. This BLOCKHEAD nurse is modeled after Andy's nurse, who was probably one of those tough old Army nurses who worked the graveyard shift from 11 p.m. to 7 a.m. Can you imagine being awakened from a sound sleep at 2 a.m. to receive a shot from this beauty. What a nightmare!

Begin by blocking in the nurse cap and bun. Accent the sunken cheeks, prominent cheek bones and scrawny neck. The legs and arms should also be thin. The left hand is in her uniform pocket. The right hand grasps the syringe. A really wicked-looking syringe can be fashioned by cutting off the head of a pin and inserting the shaft into the end of the syringe.

Props: Syringe (enema bag, rectal thermometer, optional).
Finish: Uniform, shoes and cap, white. Hair, gray.

Old Harley Biker*

This BLOCKHEAD is modeled after a 1950s biker whose hero was probably James Dean. Here he is, forty years later, still hanging on to the lifestyle. Contrary to today's Harley enthusiasts who ride twenty-thousand-dollar machines and sport color-coordinated, leather outfits and all the matching accessories, this old timer still wears the steel-toed boots, faded Levis, leather jacket, T-shirt and German-style helmet.

This one is easy to carve since the eyes are covered and the hands are in the pockets. Block in the helmet so that it fits down over the eyes. The nose is large and broad. The beard should be full with a mustache that covers the upper lip. The hair flows backward as if trained that way by wind in his face. The hands are in the jacket pockets. The legs are skinny and the Levis are rolled up. In contrast, the boots are large and have buckles on the side.

Props: Iron cross (chains, optional).
Finish: Helmet, boots and jacket, black. T-shirt, black. Jeans, denim. Hair, gray.

Orthodontist

The orthodontist was carved as a good-natured joke for my carving buddy, Dave Dunham. I wanted an orthodontist who needed some orthodontic work of his own, hence the mouth full of crooked teeth. Dave once bragged that with the right tools he could straighten any set of teeth, so I gave him a pair of large pliers and a ballpeen hammer.

The head is turned to the right. The most prominent feature is the mouth and misaligned teeth. Create a large oval mound. Draw in a big asymmetrical smile. Carve the plane for the teeth and gums. If you haven't carved gums on a carving before, just draw in the gum line and teeth, carve the gum line where it meets the teeth, and then the crooked teeth. Both hands are the same grasping/clenched type holding the hammer and pliers. The feet are balanced.

Props: Ballpeen hammer, pliers.
Finish: Shoes, black. Pants, Navy. Shirt, blue. Hair, gray.

Photographer

Photographers and woodcarvers have a lot of things in common: They come in all shapes and sizes; they are usually more interested in their hobby than in their personal appearance; and both are avid collectors of any new tools or gadgets that come long. The more props you can attach to this photographer the better. Two or three camera bodies, a light meter, rolls of film, tripod, flash units, gadget bags with lots of pockets, lenses, filters...

Carve the cap backward so as not to interfere with the camera. Block in lots of unruly hair. The face is somewhat round in shape. The left hand is a grasping/holding type. The right hand is an inward-turned palm-down holding hand. The thumb and forefinger are separated to hold the film. Feet are balanced. The camera can be carved as one piece, but it is easier to carve between the hands if it's an added item.

Props: Camera, tripod, film.

Finish: Shirt, green. Vest, tan. Cap, black with gold Canon logo. Jeans, denim. Shoes, white.

Pilgrim

The Pilgrims, being strict Puritans, were pretty low key and conservative in fashion and conduct. This Pilgrim certainly dresses in the typical somber black and white clothing. His demeanor may be a little suspect though. His face is probably a little too joyous for a pious Pilgrim. Maybe it is the vices of gluttony and drunkenness so evident in his hands that produced the smile during the Thanksgiving celebration.

The straight-brimmed Pilgrim hat can be bandsawed to shape. This brim will be fragile, so exercise caution as you thin it. Create a large oval mound for the ear to ear smile. The eyes are just narrow smiling eyes. The hair is shoulder length so the ears will be covered. The hands are both grasping-type hands.

Props: Turkey leg, tankard (blunderbuss, turkey, optional).

Finish: Suit, shoes and hat, black. Collar and socks, white. Buckles, silver.

Pirate

The nautical version of the old west out-law would have to be the pirate. A dew rag adorns his head, eye patch, short pants, striped shirt, peg leg and knife in his teeth complete the picture. The right hand holds a fist full of gold coins, no doubt looted treasure. A check in the wood caused the pirate's right foot to break off and necessitated the carving of the peg leg. Sometimes creativity comes by accident instead of planning....

The head is domed except for the knot on the dew rag. The ears are prominent. Try carving a gold ring on one ear if you want. Carve the good eye wide open as if compensating for the eye covered by the patch. Push the cheeks and smile lines well back into the face to expose the teeth that will hold the knife. The left hand rests on top of the knife sheath. The right hand is a palm-up, holding-type hand that supports the gold coins. The short pants and peg leg complete the pirate.

Props: Knife, sheath.

Finish: Dew rag, blue. Shirt, red and white. Pants, gray. Shoe, black.

Policeman

Most of us don't come in contact with the police except when we are in trouble or in violation of the law. Consequently, police officers don't always have a positive image in our minds. They are ordinary people just like us, trying to do a very difficult job. Dressing very neatly and professionally, growing a mustache and wearing mirrored sunglasses is a standard approach to looking more intimidating. "Walk softly and carry a big stick," is their philosophy.

The head is turned to his right. The hat looks better if the sides are drooping down to the ears. The brim is far down on the forehead to conceal the eyes and sunglasses. The right hand is over the gun holster; the left hand is a grasping hand holding the night stick. The feet are balanced and straight ahead.

Props: Night stick (traffic ticket pad, equipment added to the belt, optional).

Finish: Uniform, Navy. Shoes and belt, black. Mirrored glasses, silver with Ceramcoat Satin Acrylic Varnish #7007.

Redneck

Redneck Bubbas are common here in the south, but they can be found in every locale. They are called by different names: hicks, goobers, white trash.... But being a redneck is more of a state of mind or a way of life than just a name. Most are hard-working, blue-collar types just doing the best they can to get by. They are usually recognized by beer bellies, tattoos, toothpicks or dangling cigarettes, sleeveless shirts and gimme caps and make great caricatures.

Block in the too small gimme cap with the brim turned up. There is lots of shaggy hair extending down to the shoulders. The expression is dull and stupid with drooping eyelids, broad nose, and full, pouty lips from which hangs a toothpick. The exposed beer belly, too-short T-shirt and drooping pants are typical. Both hands are in his pockets. Tennis shoes are on his feet.
Props: Toothpick.
Finish: Cap, red. T-shirt, black. Jeans, denim. Tennis shoes, white. Hair, brown.

Santa

No collection of woodcarvings is complete without a Santa Claus. Santa carvings come in all types: Traditional American, Old World, German.... I have chosen to portray my BLOCKHEAD Santa as one in distress. He has a compass and map of where he is supposed to go. He looks perplexed, as if lost.

Block-in the head with the face turned to the right. Allow room for the tassel. Run the beard well down onto the chest. Make him a bit spoon-chested to accent the larger waistline. Stress fat cheeks by bringing in the temple area. The hair is long and extends onto the shoulders in back. Use a small veiner on the hair and beard rather than a v-tool for a more flowing look. The left hand is open between the thumb and fingers. The right hand is a palm-up holding type. The thumb and fingers are cupped around the compass. Boots are stove-topped with the pants stuffed into them.
Props: Check list or map, compass (presents, large sack, optional).
Finish: Santa suit, red and white. Boots, black. Hair and fur trim, white.

Shriner*

I'm not real sure why I chose to carve the Shriner, except that I have a friend who is a Shriner clown and that funny little hat (called a fez) fascinated me enough that I thought it would make an interesting caricature. The body of this carving is pretty generic and could be used for any character with a neck tie.

Taper the head and fez up to the flat top. Leave wood for the tassel hanging off the back side. The nose is very broad, as is his smile. Push the cheeks and smile lines well back into the face to make room for the oral mound with its big smile. Carve the upper and lower teeth planes. Show the gum line on the upper planes. The eyes are almost squinted closed by the big smile. Brows are arched. The body is balanced with hands in the pockets and feet straight ahead. The wide, oversized tie extends all the way over the belt.
Props: None.
Finish: Shirt, white. Tie, blue. Pants, gray. Shoes and belt, black. Fez, maroon.

Snow Skier

With all the jokes about skiing being so dangerous, this Blockhead could have a leg cast, arm sling, bandaged head and broken skis. I decided to take a more positive approach. This skier has an intense psyched-up gaze that would suggest he is anticipating the big run on the advanced course, or maybe he has just viewed the steep downhill run.

Block in the head and cap. Another option for you non-face carvers is a full-face ski mask. Leave wood for the scarf around his neck. His body shape is rather bulky since he has on warm ski clothing. The boots are smooth and aerodynamic except for the ski bindings. The hands are both grasping/holding types with bulky gloves covering most of the detail. The skis and poles are carved separately. Remember that the angle of the feet must take in consideration the extended length of the skis.
Props: Skis, poles (leg cast, arm sling, crutches, optional).
Finish: Ski suit, blue. Scarf, red. Boots, blue. Skis, red. Hair, brown.

Teacher

Teachers have certainly changed over the years. My recollection of teachers way back when I was a pupil was that they were real old, old enough to remember Noah and the Great Flood. At least they all seemed that old to my young mind. Many had a reputation as being strict or mean and could easily strike fear into the heart of any less-than-diligent student. This BLOCK-HEAD teacher is modeled after my fourth grade teacher. I'm sure she was not really this ugly, intimidating or stern-looking, but to a ten-year-old all teachers are ogres.

This BLOCKHEAD is from a band-saw blank. Remove less wood from between the legs to allow for the dress. She has a full head of hair. The left hand is in her skirt pocket, and the right hand is holding/grasping a yard stick or pointer. The feet are slightly staggered under the skirt.

Props: Yard stick/pointer (report card, whip, optional).

Finish: Dress, turquoise. Shoes, black. Hair, brown.

IN THE COLLECTION OF RACHEL SCHMIDT, FORT WORTH TX

Tennis Player

This tennis player appears to be preparing to toss the ball as he goes into his serve. This carving is a fairly traditional, old-fashioned tennis player in a neat, white outfit. Today's professional players have sponsors' logos plastered all over them like bumper stickers. This BLOCKHEAD offers a different challenge because of the angle of the head and open mouth.

Begin by blocking in the head and neck. Remember that the head is looking upward. The angle of the jaw and top of the head are critical. Leave wood for unruly hair and the head band or visor as you block-in the head. The mouth is open, and the eyes roll upward. The palm-up, holding left hand supports the ball and is against the body. The right hand, a clenched/grasping type, holds the tennis racket and is away from the body. The legs are thin, and the feet are staggered with left foot being farther forward.

Props: Tennis racket (bag, optional).

Finish: Clothing, white. Hair, brown.

IN THE COLLECTION OF FRANK ELDRED, ALBUQUERQUE, NM

Viking

The Vikings are known as fierce Scandinavian warriors who raided the coast of Europe during the 8th, 9th and 10th centuries. This Viking is dressed in stereotypical, though not authentic, viking clothes. The leather leggings and wrapped shoes are correct, as is the tunic and wool shirt. But according to the research I did, Vikings never wore helmets with horns on them. Yet this is the most recognizable article of clothing for the Vikings as we know them today. The shield and battle ax are added items, as are the horns on the helmet.

Carve the helmet first, making it too small for the head, which will accent lots of unruly hair coming from underneath it. Add the horns last. The hands are hollowed, clenched fists to hold the ax and shield. The face has a dull, stupid look with drooping eyes and an asymmetrical mustache and buck teeth.
Props: Sword, battle ax, shield, horns (mace, ball and chain, optional).
Finish: Leggings, tan. Shoes and hair, brown. Tunic, gray. Shirt and belt, black. Helmet, silver.

Volleyball Player

The inspiration for this carving came from my older daughter who requested that I carve a volleyball player, and of course, it had to be a girl. Ugly, old cowboys are more my forte than feminine caricatures, but daughters can be persistent and persuasive, so here it is–my attempt at a young female caricature.

The face is heart-shaped. The hair is pulled away from the face in a French braid that hangs down the back. There is very little brow ridge on the female face, and the oral mound protrudes more. A short, upturned nose is appropriate. A lot of wood will need to be removed from the body to give it a more feminine shape and to expose the volleyball. The volleyball could be carved as a separate piece. The right hand is a relaxed closed hand; the left supports the ball. The legs are thin with bulky, protective knee pads. She is wearing tennis-type athletic shoes.
Props: (Equipment bag, optional.)
Finish: Uniform, colors of your choice. Shoes, white. Hair yellow.

Witch

If you carve a BLOCKHEAD for one daughter, then you must carve one for the other daughter. So, Erin, this one is for you. Traditionally, witches have been portrayed as secretive, evil, ugly, old women. Halloween, dark starless nights, flying brooms, black cats, spells and boiling cauldrons are all associated with witches. I have chosen a pumpkin Jack O'Lantern and flying broom as props for this hag.

The witch is carved from a bandsaw blank with wood left between the legs to form the long gown. I also cut out the profile for the face and hat. Block in the pointed hat and floppy brim. Hair should be long and hang over the shoulder either in front or back. The left hand is grasping the flying broom. The right hand is a palm-down, holding hand. The shoes peek out from under the long gown. Don't forget the warts on the nose or chin.

Props: Broom, pumpkin.

Finish: Cap, gown and shoes, shades of black. Hair, gray or black gray or white. Jack O'Lantern, orange and black.

Wizard

The mysterious magic of the Wizard of Oz or Merlyn the Magician still stirs the imagination of children today. Their magic was mesmerizing and generally benign as compared to the villainous versions of today. This BLOCKHEAD Wizard is fairly innocent-looking with his magic scepter and crystal ball.

The wizard is carved from a bandsaw blank with wood left between the legs. I also bandsawed the painted cap that is tilted back on his head. The face and beard are full in contrast to the small cap. The hair is shoulder length and flowing. The left hand is a clenched fist type, and the right hand is a palm-up, holding hand. There is enough wood to carve the crystal ball from the blank, but I chose to carve it separately. The robe should be flowing with gentle rolls rather than straight or stiff. The shoes are barely exposed from under the robe.

Props: Scepter/wand, crystal ball.

Finish: Robe and hat, purple with gold. Shoes, brown. Hair, gray and white.

Woodcarver (Female)

While female woodcarvers are definitely a minority in numbers, they are not a minority in quality of carving. This female BLOCKHEAD woodcarver is modeled after one of the best female woodcarvers I know. Her energetic, lively style of teaching and ever-present smile and laughter make her readily recognizable. I hope that my caricature carving of her will do her justice, and that you can recognize her.

If you want to put a skirt on this figure, don't bandsaw between the legs. The hands and feet are positioned the same as the male woodcarver below; just carve them smaller and more feminine. The chisel and small animal carving are inserted. Carve a heart-shaped face surrounded by plenty of wood to style the hair. Use a veiner or deep gouge to form the hair. Carve the eyes a little larger than on male faces. Include a big smile.

Props: Chisel, carving blank (knife, mallet, optional).

Finish: Hair, dark brown. Blouse, yellow. Skirt, turquoise. Shoes, white.

IN THE COLLECTION OF DESIREE HAJNY, WICHITA, KS

Woodcarver (Male)

If you know me, you'll probably recognize this BLOCKHEAD. He has my official carving uniform of a comfortable shirt, overalls and walking shoes. When it was suggested that I do a BLOCKHEAD woodcarver, my wife said I should carve a self-portrait. Maybe she knows me well enough to equate me with a BLOCKHEAD. This carving is actually a BLOCKHEAD carving a BLOCKHEAD.

This one is pretty basic if you have carved some of the preceding BLOCKHEADS. The right hand is a clenched, grasping hand holding a knife, and the left hand is a palm-up, holding hand supporting the blank. Both the knife and the blank are carved separately. The head is round and full especially with the beard. Feet are balanced and straight ahead.

Try doing your own self-portrait. It's a challenge to analyze your own features and then to caricaturize yourself.

Props: Knife, BLOCKHEAD blank.

Finish: Shoes, blue and white. Overalls, denim. Shirt, light blue. Hair, gray.

IN THE COLLECTION OF PATRICIA K. PRESCOTT, FORT WORTH, TX

Chapter 7

Blockhead Props

IN THIS CHAPTER YOU WILL FIND PATTERNS FOR PROPS ADDED TO THE BLOCKHEADS in Chapter 6. The 51 BLOCKHEAD projects presented in Chapter 6 are listed below in alphabetical order. The props that are used with each caricature are listed behind each project. Use the numbers to match up the patterns with the project. Optional prop patterns are in parentheses. Some prop patterns can be interchanged. The use of these and other added items in a small scene can greatly enhance the visual impact and appeal of your BLOCKHEAD.

1. Auto Mechanic–wrench, repair bill, (tool box)
2. Barnstormer Pilot
3. Baseball Player
4. Basketball Player
5. Boxer
6. Canadian Mountie
7. Carpenter/Woodworker–hammer
8. Caveman–club
9. Cavewoman
10. Civil War Soldier– sword, scabbard, (rifle, flag)
11. Clown
12. coach–clipboard
13. Cowboy
14. Deep Sea Diver–Buoy knife, sea horse
15. Dentist–diopters, pliers with tooth
16. Doctor–pencil, file folder
17. Fireman–hose, axe
19. Fisherman–fish

20. Frankenstein
21. Friar Tuck–staff, turkey leg
22. Frontiersman–knife, scabbard, (rifle)
23. Golfer–bent club, score card
24. Hockey Player–stick, skate blades
25. Hunter–shotgun
26. Indian Brave–bow, arrow, feathers
27. Keystone Cop–night stick
28. Leprechaun–cane
29. Little Old Man–cane
30. Lumberjack–ax, tree
31. Magician–magic wand, rabbit in hat
32. Modern Airline Pilot–map, travel bag
33. Nurse–syringe, (enema bag)
34. Old Harley Biker
35. Orthodontist–hammer, pliers, (come along hitch)

36. Photographer–camera, tripod, (bags)
37. Pilgrim–turkey leg, tankard, (blunderbuss)
38. Pirate–knife, scabbard
39. Policeman–night stick
40. Redneck–toothpick
41. Santa–checklist
42. Shriner
43. Snow Skier
44. Teacher–ruler or pointer, report card
45. Tennis Player–racquet
46. Viking–sword, shield, horns
47. Volleyball Player
48. Witch–broom, Jack-O-Lantern
49. Wizard–crystal ball, wand
50. Woodcarver (male)–knife, Blockhead carving (chisel or mallet)
51. Woodcarver (female)–knife, animal carving (chisel or mallet)

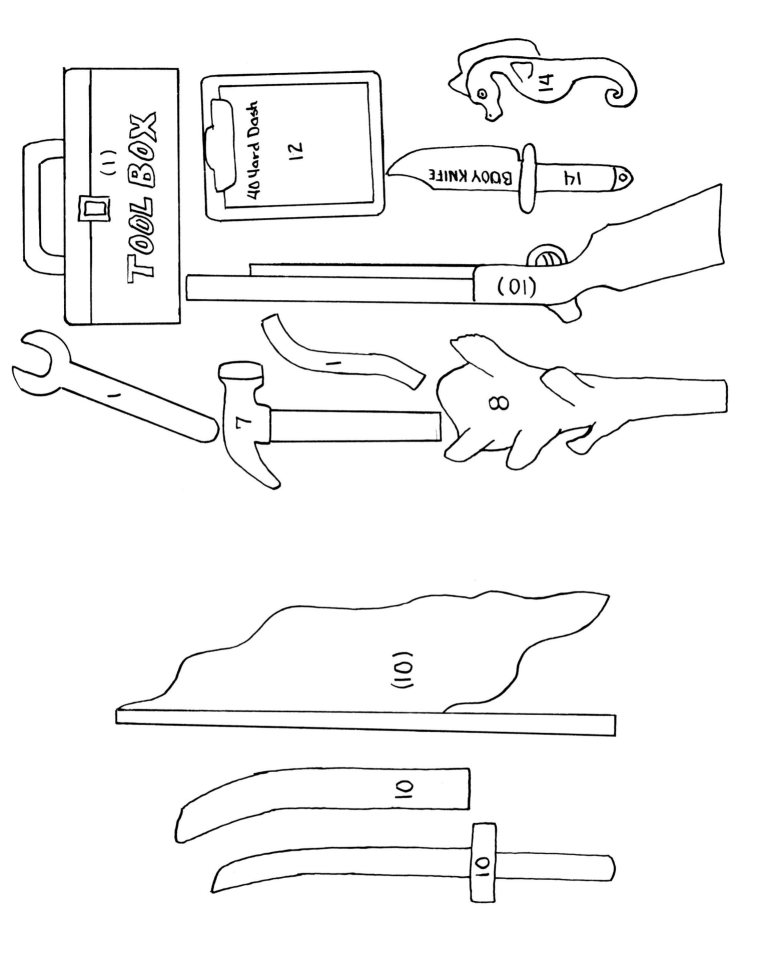

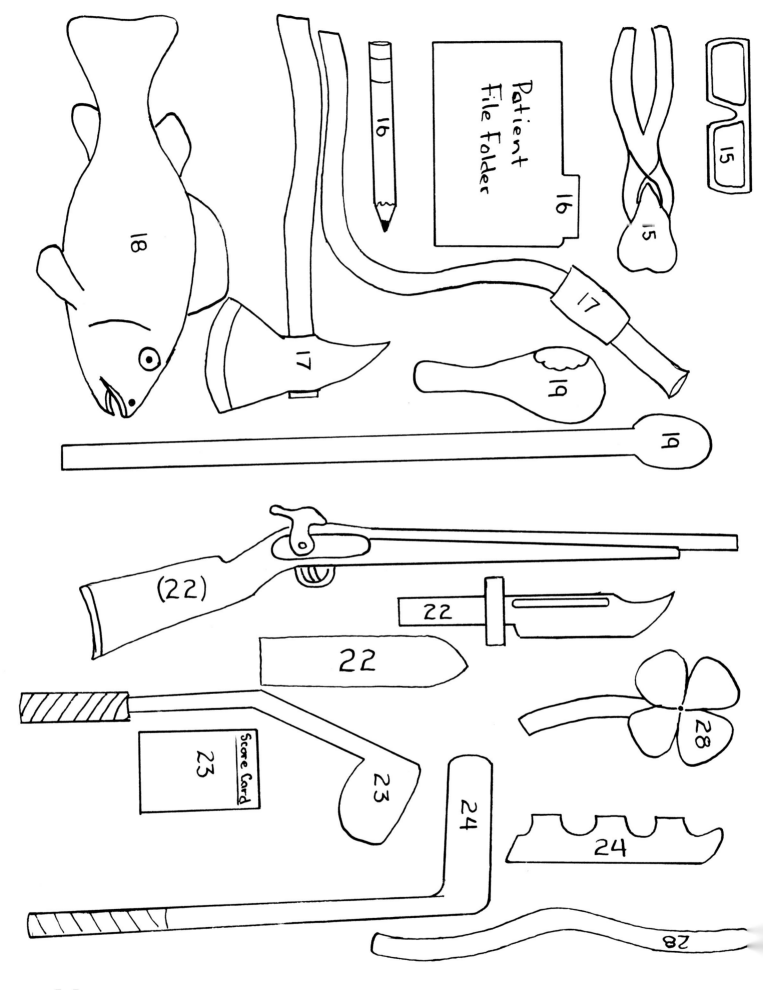

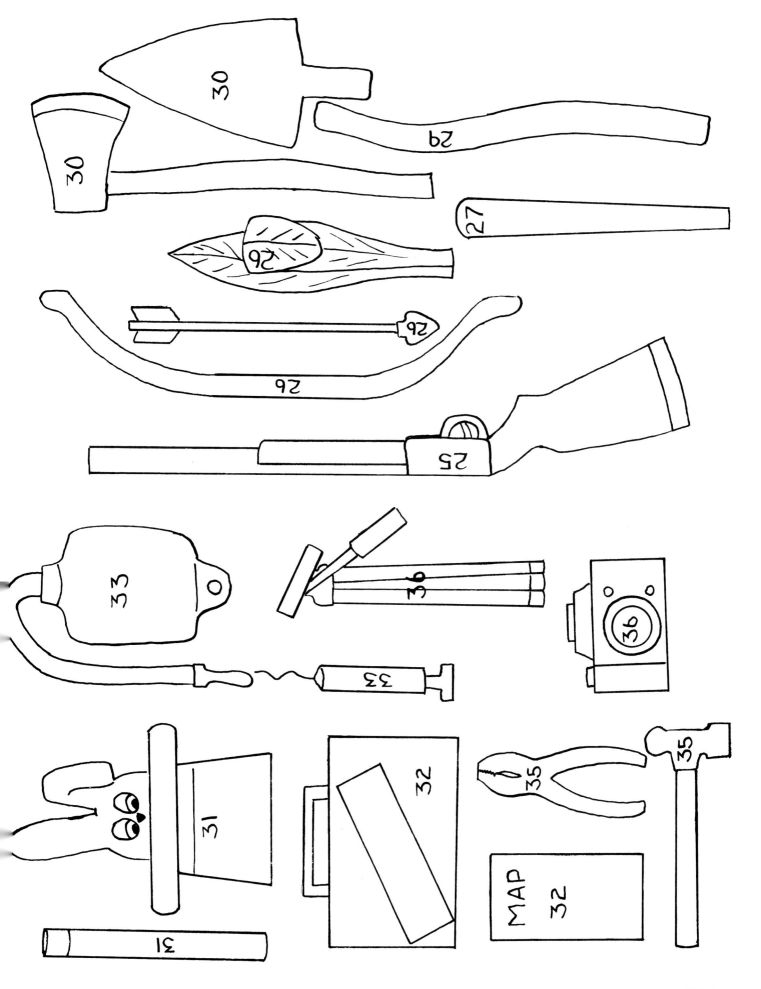

30

29

30

27

26

26

26

25

33

36

36

33

31

32

32

35

35

31

MAP
32

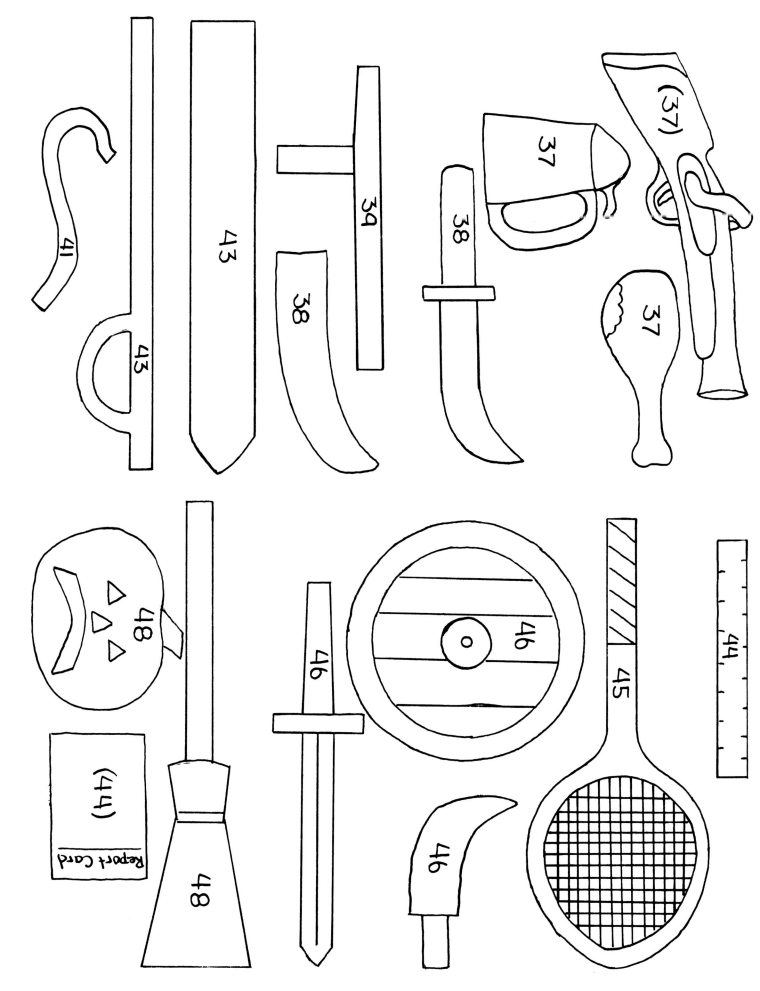

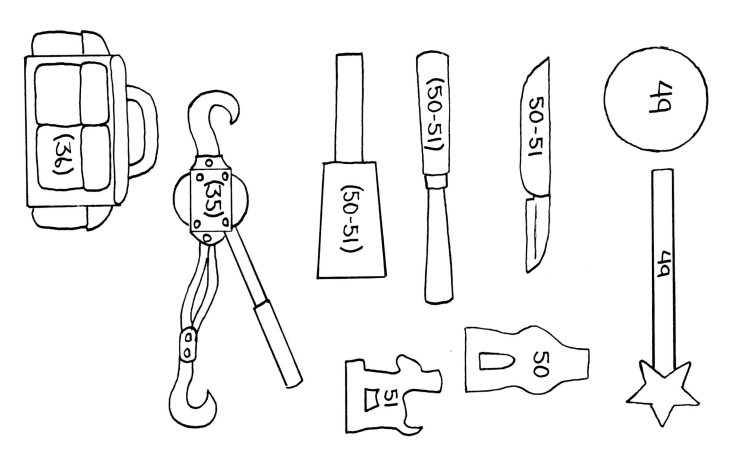

Afterword

In writing this book, my goal was to stimulate some creative ideas in you. I hope we have both been successful in achieving that goal. Be brave, try new ideas. Hopefully you can use this book to climb to a new plateau in your carving skills. I am very interested in seeing your new BLOCKHEAD creations. If you'll send me a photograph of your ideas, I'll send you a certificate as an Official BLOCKHEAD Carver.

In conclusion, let me say thank you to several people who helped make this book possible. Thanks for the fantastic carvings shared by my carving friends who were featured in the "Guest Carvers Photo Gallery." I wish I could have kept them instead of only photographing them. Thanks to all my students and friends who have encouraged me in this effort and have had the patience of Job waiting for it to be completed. Thanks to my wife, Pat, whose skills on the computer, encouragement, prodding, and support are invaluable. Finally, thanks to you, the reader of this book. If you have read this far, you are a special person, and you honor me by persevering through this text and even by the fact that you valued what I had to say by laying out your hard-earned money. Thank you.

Stephen H. Prescott
5812 Lalagray Lane
Fort Worth, TX 76148

Guest Carver Photo Gallery

Old Man
Pete LeClair–Massachusetts

Gnome
Joe Wannamaker–Illinois

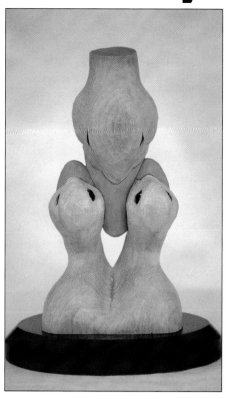

Ducks
Ted McGill–South Carolina

Fireman
Pete Ortel–New York

Sumo Wrestler
Doug Raine–Arizona

Farmer
Harley Schmitgen, Minnesota

Construction Worker
Steve Prescott–Texas

NY Cowboy
Bob Travis–California

Boobie Sue II
Dave Dunham–Texas

Scout Master
Bob Goss–California

Santa Wolf with Teddy
Desiree Hajny–Kansas

Football Player
Randy Landen–Kansas

You are invited to Join the

National Wood Carvers Association
"Some carve their careers: others just chisel"
since 1953

If you have any interest in woodcarving: if you carve wood, create wood sculpture or even just whittle in your spare time, you will enjoy your membership in the National Wood Carvers Association. The non-profit NWCA is the world's largest carving club with over 33,000 members. There are NWCA members in more than 56 countries around the globe.

The Association's goals are to:
- promote wood carving
- foster fellowship among member enthusiasts
- encourage exhibitions and area get togethers
- list sources of equipment and information for the wood carving artist
- provide a forum for carving artists

The NWCA serves as a valuable network of tips, hints and helpful information for the wood carver. Membership is only $11.00 per year.

Members receive the magazine "Chip Chats" six times a year, free with their membership. "Chip Chats" contains articles, news events, demonstrations of technique, patterns and a full color section showcasing examples of fine craftsmanship. Through this magazine you will be kept up to date on shows and workshops to attend, new products, special offers to NWCA members and other members' activities in your area and around the world.

National Wood Carvers Association
7424 Miami Ave.
Cincinnati, OH 45243

Name: _____

Address: _____

_____

Dues $11.00 per year in USA, $14.00 per year foreign (payable in US Funds)